STRAIGHT TALKING

Marijuana

Sean Connolly

A+

Smart Apple Media

Published by Smart Apple Media
2140 Howard Drive West
North Mankato, MN 56003

Designed by Guy Callaby
Edited by Pip Morgan
Artwork by Karen Donnelly
Picture research by Cathy Tatge

Photograph acknowledgements

Photographs by Alamy (Edward Parker), Guy Callaby, Getty Images
(Michael L. Abramson / Time Life Pictures, Daniel Arsenault, Neil
Beckerman, Per-Eric Berglund, Bruno Press, Peter Cade, Matt Cardy,
Christopher Bissel, Bill Crump, Marco Di Lauro, JAY DIRECTO / AFP,
Julia Fullerton-Batten, RAMZI HAIDAR / AFP, Jo Hale, Sandy Huffaker,
Hulton Archive, Maike Jessen, Erica Lansner, Ron Levine, Don
MacKinnon, Mario Magnani / Liaison, Mansell / Time Life Pictures,
Greg Marinovich, Doug Menuez, Gilles Mingasson / Liaison, Natalie
Pecht, ADALBERTO ROQUE / AFP, Rosebud Pictures, Fredrik Skold,
Simon Songhurst, Sion Touhig, Donald Weber, Ron Wurzer)

Printed in China

Library of Congress Cataloging-in-Publication Data

Connolly, Sean.
Marijuana / by Sean Connolly.
p. cm. — (Straight talking)
Includes index.
ISBN-13: 978-1-58340-647-2
1. Marijuana. 2. Marijuana abuse—Prevention.
I. Title.

HV5822.M3C645 2006
613.8'35—dc22   2006001429

First Edition

9 8 7 6 5 4 3 2 1

Contents

These unusual sunglasses show the distinctive leaves of the marijuana plant.

Have you ever been fed up or worried and felt like putting your cares aside for a while? Or maybe you and your friends noticed something funny together and shared a moment of laughter. Marijuana is a drug that seems to give people these relaxed and happy times. It certainly changes the way people see and feel things.

Marijuana is the most common illegal drug in the world. Millions of people of all ages smoke it regularly, and most began taking it when they were young. Have you ever been at a party where you saw people passing a cigarette between them, each inhaling a lungful of smoke that had a distinctive smell? Perhaps you have even been offered one of these joints and were tempted to say yes. This book will help you understand what marijuana is, what it can do to you, and who takes it and why.

A little boost

People often turn to substances to help them relax, cover up their worries, or prolong their pleasure. Many adults drink alcohol as a way of loosening up or giving themselves a little boost. Other people prefer to smoke marijuana because they find that this makes boring things seem a little more bearable, and even funny.

A lot of people have come to believe that taking marijuana is a safer way of relaxing than drinking alcohol. Some actually grow it themselves. In the United Kingdom (UK), about 60 percent of the marijuana smoked is grown at home and not brought in from other countries. People sell and trade seeds for different types of marijuana such as skunk, which can be up to 10 times more powerful than traditional marijuana.

Meeting for a drink is a popular way for people to unwind or celebrate. The only drug many people use for this purpose is alcohol.

A hidden price

You may have heard the saying "there's no such thing as a free lunch." It means that there is usually a hidden price to pay for something that seems—at first—to be good. It would be great fun to be able to switch on a good mood whenever you want to and keep it on for a few hours. But marijuana changes the way the brain works, although it is unclear how damaging this change might be—even after many years of research. Some scientists fear that by smoking marijuana regularly, people risk permanent damage to their memory.

Another big concern is that marijuana can make you feel bad. Some people try marijuana once and feel frightened and disturbed, so they vow never to try it again. Others might take it when their brain is already struggling to overcome depression or schizophrenia; for them, the marijuana experience could be very frightening.

SEARCHING QUESTION
Marijuana is sometimes sold and even smoked near schools and playgrounds. Would you recognize what was happening if you saw people smoking it? Would you be able to tell whether a person was smoking marijuana or an ordinary cigarette?

Marijuana basics

Marijuana plants sprouting buds in the wild. If they have enough sunshine and water, marijuana plants can reach a height of 20 feet (6 m).

HOW MARIJUANA IS SOLD

Marijuana leaves are dried and sold in clear bags. Dried buds, which contain more THC than the leaves, are sometimes mixed in. The bags are sold by weight: in the United States, bags are usually sold by the ounce (28 g), half ounce (14 g), quarter ounce (7 g), and so on. Dealers in Australia and other countries sell it in multiples of grams. In 2005, U.S. marijuana users paid $60 to $600 for a one-ounce (28 g) bag, while in Australia, a one-gram (0.04 oz.) bag of marijuana cost $11 to $19.

Marijuana, or *Cannabis sativa*, grows naturally in many parts of the world. There is nothing very unusual about the appearance of this plant, apart from its narrow, serrated leaves, which you may have seen on the front of some T-shirts. For many years, the plant has been a source of tough fibers (known as hemp), which are used to make rope, twine, and textiles.

The leaves and buds of the marijuana plant are the most important for those who smoke marijuana because of the chemicals they contain. The chief active ingredient is delta-9 tetrahydrocannabinol (THC for short), which is a drug that can change a person's mood. Once THC enters the brain, it creates changes in the way people behave and experience things. This is known as "getting high."

A long history

People have known about the properties of marijuana for more than 4,000 years. According to historical evidence, marijuana was used as a medicine in India, China, and parts of the Middle East. Chinese doctors treated malaria, rheumatism, and other illnesses with marijuana. Elsewhere, it was used to dull people's aches and pains.

Europeans first learned of its painkilling properties in the late Middle Ages from traders who traveled from the Middle East and Asia. People drank marijuana in the form of a tincture but did not usually smoke it. By the 19th century, such marijuana preparations were sold legally in many countries. In England, Queen Victoria's doctor even recommended it to her to reduce the pain of menstrual cramps.

By the end of the 1800s, marijuana fell from favor as a medicine—partly because other painkillers, such as aspirin, were introduced. However, people had discovered the drug's other properties—it seemed to create feelings of pleasure and made people feel good. A new chapter in marijuana use was about to begin.

❝ When pure and administered carefully, [marijuana is] one of the of the most valuable medicines we possess. ❞

Queen Victoria's personal physician, Sir Russell Reynolds, describing marijuana in the first issue of the British medical journal *The Lancet* (1890).

These Vietnamese women display fabrics made with hemp fibers and dyed with indigo.

Naga Babas, or Hindu holy men, smoke hashish regularly and especially during rites at the Kumbh Mela Festival every year. They are followers of the Hindu god Shiva, who is considered to be the god of hashish.

How people take marijuana

Most marijuana users smoke a mixture of dried leaves and flowers. They crumble the mixture into a cigarette paper and roll it into a homemade cigarette, known as a joint. They may mix the marijuana with tobacco to make the joint burn more smoothly, or smoke the leaf-flower mixture in pipes called chillums or water pipes (bongs). They inhale the smoke deeply and hold it in their lungs for a few seconds—the THC enters the bloodstream quickly and soon reaches the brain.

Marijuana resin is also smoked. When it is removed from the plant, the resin is like the sap of an evergreen tree. As it hardens, it is formed into sticky balls, firmer blocks, or flakes, which vary in color from light brown to deep black. This is known as hashish. It can also be made by compressing the pollen from the flowers.

Some hashish contains higher amounts of THC than the leaves and flowers, so the effects of smoking it may be greater. However, a few powerful strains of marijuana leaves can match the THC levels of hashish. Hashish can be made stronger yet by boiling it in certain chemicals to produce a liquid known as hash oil. This oil can contain up to 25 times more THC than marijuana leaves.

Leaves, buds, hashish, and hash oil can also be cooked and eaten. One way is to add the marijuana to a cake or cookie mixture. Marijuana in cookies, cakes, and brownies takes longer to have an effect, as the THC is only released once the food is digested. This delay can carry a risk— people might think they haven't used enough marijuana and eat more, and then have a bad experience when the drug finally reaches the brain.

A storekeeper displays bongs (water pipes) and other products related to marijuana smoking.

Charles Baudelaire, the famous 19th-century French poet, drew this self-portrait under the influence of hashish.

No one knows how many people used marijuana for pleasure in the 19th century. Some famous people readily talked about their experiences. In the early 1800s, some English poets and writers admitted to using opium, a stronger drug that leads to dream-filled sleep.

By the middle of the century, hashish had become popular with French artists and writers. In the 1850s, some of them formed the hashish users' club.

Feeling rebellious

During the 20th century, marijuana became a drug used by millions of people around the world. By the 1930s, most countries had made it illegal, but this didn't stop people from smoking it. As a result, it became the most widely used illegal drug in the world.

The rise in use mirrored some changes in society, especially after World War II, when the U.S. and, to a lesser extent, other Western countries became very wealthy.

Advertisements persuaded people that their lives would be better and they would be happier if they bought the products that this new wealth was able to manufacture. These included TVs, dishwashers, refrigerators, second cars, and bigger houses. People were encouraged to keep up with their neighbors and compete in a sort of race to buy the newest and biggest products.

Dropping out

Other people, including popular writers such as Jack Kerouac, believed this rat race was foolish. For them, happiness came from new experiences rather than buying more things.

By the 1960s, many young people were following the advice of Harvard University psychologist Timothy Leary, who urged them to "tune in, turn on, and drop out" of what he saw as society's boring old ways of thinking. However, most people were afraid to take LSD, the powerful drug favored by Leary. They turned to marijuana when they felt rebellious instead. Young people followed the example of many musicians, who smoked marijuana and took other drugs.

FACT

Marijuana is California's largest cash crop. Officials estimate that it is worth $3–$5 billion each year. Compare this amount with the leading legally produced crops: grapes ($2.6 billion), lettuce ($1.4 billion), and flowers ($1 billion).

During the Roaring Twenties, a decade when alcohol was outlawed in the U.S., many jazz musicians smoked marijuana instead.

DIY drugs

Marijuana has become even more popular since the 1960s, and some of the people who first smoked it as teenagers are still using it as they near retirement. Most people still consider it to be safer than other illegal drugs (and in some people's view, safer than alcohol). Another reason for its popularity is that, unlike ecstasy or cocaine, marijuana is seen as natural—it is not produced in a laboratory.

Much of the marijuana smoked around the world is homegrown, either in secret locations outdoors or inside people's homes. Most of this marijuana is used by the growers. This makes it hard for the police to control the use of the drug as they would, for example, cocaine or heroin (where supplies can be reduced by a successful police raid on dealers).

Marijuana growers trade information about growing techniques as they develop and grow new strains. In addition, they buy and sell the seeds of successful new strains. Although this buying and selling is just as illegal as buying and selling marijuana leaf or hashish, growers avoid the authorities by using mail order and exchanging information via the Internet.

Young workers harvest marijuana plants in a fertile valley in Lebanon. Marijuana is an important crop in many poor countries, even though it is illegal.

Some home growers have used intensive farming techniques to develop new strains of marijuana, such as skunk. Like farmers growing wheat, potatoes, or other crops, they are trying to develop plants that will grow quickly and produce a large harvest. The other goal for marijuana growers is to find strains that are stronger—in other words, strains that contain a higher concentration of THC.

All of this has become big business, with many growers planting marijuana in large outdoor plots or cultivating it on a large scale indoors, using special lamps to create hothouse conditions that are ideal for growing. Some growers sell seeds for strains that contain more than double the amount of THC that marijuana typically had 20 years ago. In 2005, some American drug officials were warning of new strains that contained up to 10 times more THC compared to the marijuana of the 1970s and 1980s, when many adults first tried it.

There are hundreds of slang terms to describe marijuana, its effects, how it is taken, and much more. These terms often fade from use, only to replaced by others. Here are some current terms:

Baked: *high on marijuana.*
Blaze: *to smoke marijuana.*
Cannabis: *a term for marijuana.*
Dagga: *a South African term for marijuana.*
Deal: *to sell marijuana.*
Dope: *slang for marijuana.*
Eighth: *a common amount of marijuana sold (one-eighth of an ounce, or 3.5 g).*
Ganja: *originally a Hindi term for marijuana.*
Herb: *slang for marijuana.*
Joint: *a hand-rolled marijuana cigarette (sometimes mixed with tobacco).*
Munchies: *the feeling of hunger when someone is high.*
Reefer: *slang for a joint.*
Roach: *a cardboard filter used in a joint.*
Skins: *cigarette papers used to roll joints.*
Skunk: *a wide-ranging term for powerful marijuana. It describes either a strain of the marijuana plant high in THC or the flowering tops of some marijuana plants.*
Stoned: *high on marijuana.*
Toke up: *to smoke marijuana.*
Wasted: *high on marijuana.*

Marijuana growing in intensive conditions in Stockholm, Sweden.

People find all sort of reasons to take substances that change the way they feel or behave. They might be insecure, unhappy, worried, or simply curious. They might just want to have a good time. These are all reasons why people take marijuana, just as they might choose alcohol or cocaine or ecstasy. Many people find that getting high and being high is fun. It offers a chance to see things differently and sometimes to share this experience with others.

Many young people turn to marijuana as a way of staying close to friends who use the drug.

Peer pressure

But people who smoke marijuana know it is illegal. Even if they believe it is harmless, they know that they run the risk of being caught. People who say, "it's a free country," or "no one is forcing you to smoke a joint," ignore a powerful reason why many people begin taking marijuana.

Most people first become exposed to marijuana in their teens, an age when it is very important to feel cool or part of a group. If one or more members of a group begin smoking marijuana, then others often feel the need to follow. Otherwise, they fear that they will seem cowardly or uncool. Peer pressure is the reason many people begin taking the drug.

The festival spirit

Many people describe being high as feeling mellow—a sort of good mood in which nothing seems to bother them. Troubles seem to fade away as people think more about enjoying what is happening around them. The mellow feeling is heightened among a group of friends or even with strangers who have come together for a party or some other gathering.

Music festivals have become ideal places for sharing marijuana. People pass joints to each other through the crowd and share in a group feeling of warmth and friendliness. Vendors provide festival-goers with a range of snacks and blowout meals because they know that people who are high need to eat. The feeling of being at a festival—often described as being a buzz in itself—can be another type of peer pressure. Many festival-goers feel that they are somehow losing out on the full experience if they don't join the others and smoke some joints.

Marijuana, like alcohol, can cause people to lose their inhibitions (social fears and embarrassment) when they are in a large crowd.

17

DISCOVERING SHAKESPEARE

Below, Sarah, a college student, tells about how she first took marijuana in high school.

"It was the end of my sophomore year, and I was part of a school group that went to an open-air production of Midsummer Night's Dream. We had been studying it in English, and our teacher was saying that it was really funny if you saw it (we found that hard to believe).

"Once we had found a spot for our picnic blankets, some of us went off to the bathroom. Behind some bushes near the bathroom, one of my friends then lit up a hand-rolled cigarette. She took a couple drags, then passed it on to the girl next to her. She passed it to me. I wasn't stupid, and I figured what it was from the smell and the way the girls kept looking over their shoulders to see whether anyone was watching.

"I decided to give it a try. I don't smoke, so when I took a puff, I coughed really loudly. The girls got annoyed, saying I was wasting it and attracting attention. But I tried another puff and held that one in. The joint made the rounds two or three more times, with me getting more experienced each time.

"We went back to the group just as the play was starting. I started to feel high for the first time. I got a bit distracted looking at the branches of the trees, and I was convinced I could hear every leaf rustling when there was a breeze. Then I started watching the play. I couldn't believe how funny it was. My friends and I started laughing in the first scene and kept it up to the end. Our teacher must have guessed what was up, judging by her expression, but because we seemed to be enjoying it, she didn't let on.

"I've smoked it quite a few times since then, but less now that I'm at college. Part of me still finds it fun. Another part, though, thinks that if you find everything funny, then you start to lose your judgement about what really is funny. And maybe that's not so good."

Howard Marks served seven years in an American prison for drug-dealing crimes but still campaigns for legalizing marijuana.

SEARCHING QUESTION

Sarah, the college student interviewed above, seems to be outgrowing marijuana; she now believes the reason she found so many things funny or clever was because the drug tricked her into thinking they were. Do you think she would have believed anyone who told her that before she smoked it?

FACT

The 2004 National Survey on Drug Use showed that:

● *About 40 percent of Americans over the age of 12 report that they've used marijuana at some point in their lives.*

● *About 342,000 American youths between the ages of 12 and 17 report using the drug almost daily.*

In 2004, the European Monitoring Center for Drugs and Drug Addiction found that two in five 15-year-olds in the UK had tried marijuana—more than in any other European country. About 1 in 10 in the same age group had smoked marijuana more than 40 times in the previous year.

A man openly smokes a large marijuana joint during the Marijuana March for Freedom in the Canadian capital, Ottawa, in June 2004.

Marijuana affects different people in different ways. How a person feels after smoking or eating marijuana depends on many things, such as his or her mood beforehand, how strong the marijuana is, and whether he or she also has another drug such as alcohol in his or her body. It takes only a few minutes for the THC to reach the brain if marijuana is smoked (an hour or more if it is eaten), and the high begins to wear off after a couple of hours. If a user takes more marijuana during this time, the high is usually prolonged.

Like a daydream

As the drug takes effect, users begin to experience some sights and sounds, such as music, more deeply. When they are high, or stoned, their ordinary thoughts slip away, and they may concentrate on just one sight or sound—a melody, the feel of a leaf, or cloud patterns in the sky—much like a daydream. Concentrating so hard on something sometimes makes it seem odd or terribly interesting—or just funny. It's a bit like the feeling you get when you repeat a name or a word over and over again until it becomes just a couple of funny, almost meaningless, sounds.

The sense of becoming high can be like the feeling when someone suddenly sees the image hidden in a 3-D picture, such as the one above.

INSIDE THE BRAIN

The feelings people experience when they take marijuana are caused by chemical changes in the brain. The THC attaches itself to receptors in the brain's nerve cells and changes the way information is transmitted. Some parts of the brain have more receptors than others, particularly the midbrain.

Receptors in areas of the midbrain, such as the hippocampus, septal area, and cingulate cortex (shown below), seem to be greatly affected. These are the places we store memories and feel emotions.

THC can affect the way new information is stored in the brain's long-term memory. This might explain why stoned people seem so forgetful, sometimes losing track of what they are saying in the middle of a sentence. THC may also produce sudden and profound feelings that may make the user find things funny, sad, or scary.

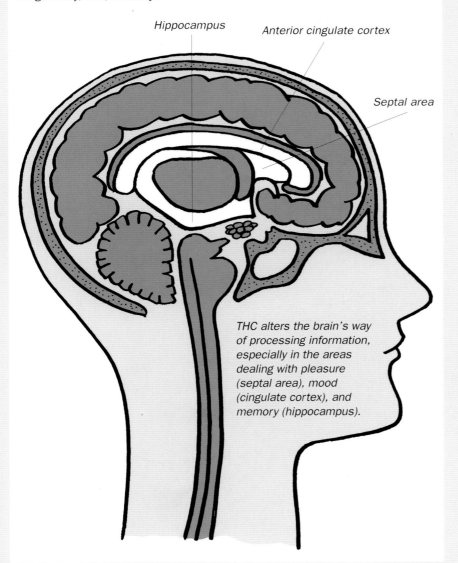

Hippocampus

Anterior cingulate cortex

Septal area

THC alters the brain's way of processing information, especially in the areas dealing with pleasure (septal area), mood (cingulate cortex), and memory (hippocampus).

↑

Marijuana fuels the munchies—a boost in appetite that gives users a powerful urge to eat their favorite foods.

Losing track of time

People who smoke or eat marijuana also lose track of time. For example, they might look at a coin for five minutes, examining the shape of the letters, the feel of the metal, the details of the picture on it, and even the clink if they drop it on the floor. They may also lose their short-term memory—within a few minutes, they could forget that they have been looking at the coin!

The munchies

A common side effect of taking marijuana is a boost to the appetite, usually referred to as the munchies. This can occur soon after taking the drug but more often occurs after about three hours, when the other effects of the drug have worn off. Scientists believe that the THC in marijuana acts on a part of the brain that stimulates the appetite, leading to a powerful craving for food.

WHAT TO LOOK FOR

Marijuana affects people in different ways, and some people have very different experiences each time they take it. Below are some of the common effects; many of them are not pleasant.

- *Dry mouth.*

- *Red eyes.*

- *Faster heartbeat.*

- *Becoming really hungry (often called the munchies).*

- *Poor memory and concentration.*

- *Confused sense of time.*

- *Changed moods.*

DEEP THOUGHTS

Gary, in his 20s, remembers how he felt the first few times he took marijuana.

"My friends and I found ourselves looking at a fashion magazine that my sister had left in the living room. None of us would ever have opened this magazine, but it was the only thing there to look at. There we were, three guys staring at stitching and colors, talking about the shape of shoes—that sort of thing. One of us said that without the dope, we would never have been able to appreciate these things. He got a pencil and paper and started writing down some of our comments because we felt we'd be glad to look at them later. Somehow, we managed to lose the piece of paper, but my mother found it a couple of days later. I took it and found that all that was written on it was 'even models have two feet.' Pretty deep, eh?"

Along a scary path

Marijuana users who concentrate hard and see things in a different way from normal might believe that they are coming up with deep thoughts and important new ways of looking at life (see panel, left). But this concentration, while harmless or funny at times, can also take users along a frightening path. They might begin thinking about things that had worried them before taking the marijuana—a homework project, whether a friend really likes them, or whether some passers-by have reported them to the police. This sort of intense worry can lead to a form of paranoia, which is a strong feeling that the world is against you.

Driving while high on marijuana is dangerous because the driver is less able to judge what is happening and may even become paranoid about being followed.

This woman's badge shows that she supports the campaign to make marijuana legal.

People who take any mood-changing drug over a long period of time will be affected by changes to their health. The effects differ from person to person. Some people can carry on with their lives, feeling no ill effects. For others, the long-term effects can be troubling—physically, psychologically, and socially.

Physical effects

People who smoke marijuana are likely to experience some of the problems linked to tobacco smoking. Although most regular marijuana users don't smoke nearly as many joints as tobacco smokers do cigarettes, joints are more harmful. Scientists calculate that some of the cancer-causing ingredients of a cigarette, especially tar, are highly concentrated in joints. Smoke, whether from tobacco or marijuana, irritates breathing passages and lungs, causing wheezing and coughing.

Prolonged marijuana use can lead to more serious breathing illnesses, such as bronchitis, pneumonia, and even lung cancer. Scientific studies of animals show that THC harms the body's immune system, so people are more likely to catch colds and other infections. Studies in the U.S. support this: because of health problems, regular marijuana smokers missed more days of school and work than nonsmokers.

" Marijuana contains more than 400 chemicals, including most of the harmful substances found in tobacco smoke. Smoking one marijuana cigarette deposits about four times more tar into the lungs than a filtered tobacco cigarette. "

Greater Dallas (Texas) Council on Alcohol and Drug Abuse.

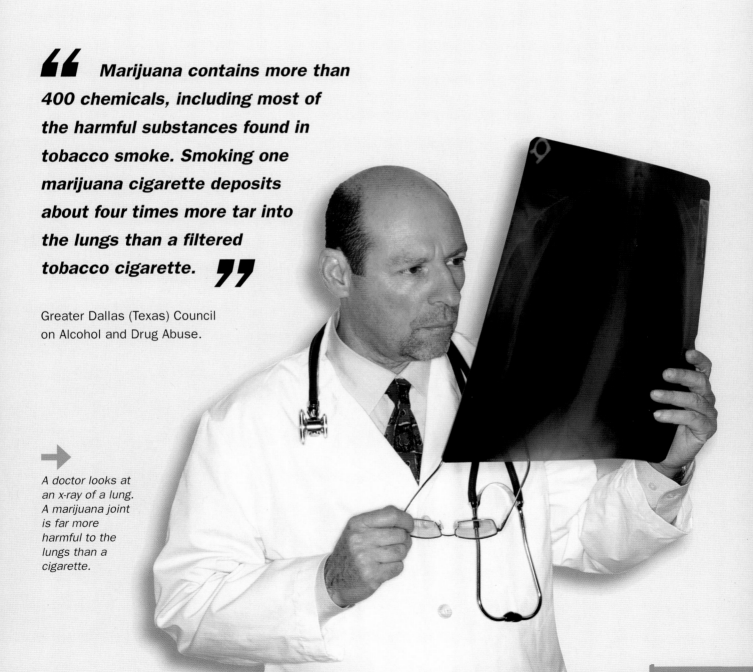

→

A doctor looks at an x-ray of a lung. A marijuana joint is far more harmful to the lungs than a cigarette.

Mental muddles

Over the past 30 years or so, as marijuana use has become more widespread, people have noticed that some regular marijuana users seem to be vague and uninterested in things. They lose interest in trying new activities or in pushing themselves at school or at work. It's as if they are in a mental muddle and saying "Who cares?"

Psychologists have a term to describe this type of behavior—amotivational syndrome. People need to be motivated, to have a determination that drives them to do their best. One danger of marijuana is that many users lose this inner drive and seem to prefer escaping from reality. This is especially dangerous for young people, who need qualifications in order to find interesting and satisfying jobs in later life.

Medical students learn about the long-term health effects of marijuana during their years of training to become doctors.

Chilling out is a novelty at first, but it can become the main activity of people who use marijuana over a long period.

No one knows what causes this loss of drive, but it might be linked to the action of THC on the brain's ability to process information. Other psychological effects of long-term marijuana use are more serious and frightening, and may cause deeper trouble, such as schizophrenia or even psychosis.

Research into the psychological effects of marijuana can be confusing. It is hard to be sure that marijuana directly causes deep psychological problems, but many people believe there is a link. In October 2005, Dr. Thomas Stuttaford wrote in *The Times* that "a person who suffers a psychotic breakdown after marijuana, had he not smoked it, might well have journeyed happily through life being no more than mildly eccentric."

❝ It just messes with your head. I had to sleep with a knife under my bed because I used to think people were going to come in and bash me during the night or something. Just for my marijuana or something, yeah. ❞

Danni, 17, interviewed on *Messing With Heads*, shown on ABC (Australia) TV, March 7, 2005.

SEARCHING QUESTION
Some supporters of marijuana suggest that users who develop psychosis might have become that way even without taking marijuana. Opponents say that might be true, but that "might" is the important word, and even a small risk is not worth taking. What do you think?

For many users, taking marijuana becomes part of a routine when they meet other people. What starts out as an escape can turn into a habit.

One of the big questions surrounding marijuana—and any drug, whether legal or illegal—is whether it is habit-forming. Are people driven to take it more and more often, even if they know they shouldn't? To answer this, we need to understand the nature of dependence.

Experts talk about two types of drug dependence: physical dependence and psychological dependence. Either (or both) of these can develop after a person takes a drug regularly and develops a habit. And either (or both) can exert a powerful hold on people.

Heroin and alcohol are good examples of drugs that lead to physical dependence: the body becomes so accustomed to having the drug that

Long-term users of marijuana become experts at rolling joints wherever they happen to be.

it depends on having it. When the drug is withdrawn (taken away), the person has a powerful and unpleasant experience known as withdrawal. Marijuana can produce a mild type of withdrawal. Another feature of physical dependence is the need to take more of the drug in order to reach the same high. This is sometimes the case with marijuana, but not nearly as much as with heroin.

Psychological dependence describes a person's need to use a drug just to feel normal. Marijuana does not seem to cause this feeling in the way that other drugs, such as alcohol or tobacco, do. However, it can make people want to take it again and again. Many regular users feel that marijuana is an important part of their daily lives and is the only way they can relax, unwind, deal with unhappiness, or simply deal with everyday events. Also, some of the effects marijuana produces—especially making boring things seem funny or interesting—make some people become irritable when they are not high.

Sam (not his real name) has been a regular marijuana user for 30 years. He was studying to be a doctor but was expelled for smoking marijuana instead of going to class. He now works as a handyman.

"I managed to study hard at school and at college, even though I was smoking pretty regularly—three or four times a week. It kind of got on top of me after a while, as if something was going to have to go.

"I started skipping classes at college, but I think some of the instructors saw me looking pretty red-eyed and out of it when I should have been in classes.

"It sucked being dumped by the university, especially when my friends were getting degrees. I kept on smoking, though, maybe to help me forget the whole experience. It seemed at that point that the dope had become part of my life. And I guess it's stayed that way since. I keep thinking of new things to do, but in the end, it just seems easier to light up and turn off for a while."

Regular marijuana users often have bloodshot (red) eyes because THC increases the flow of blood into the capillaries in the eyes.

DECIDING FOR THEMSELVES

Many drug counselors believe that users have to decide for themselves whether or not they are dependent on marijuana. People are more likely to change their behavior if they have decided something for themselves. Users might be asked to draw up two lists: "What I like about marijuana" and "What I don't like about marijuana." Then they are asked to check which list is longer. Doing this regularly helps some people to realize that they have become dependent on marijuana.

Typical lists might include the following:

WHAT I LIKE ABOUT MARIJUANA

● It makes me feel mellow.

● Dull things are more interesting and maybe even funny.

● It's fun to take with friends.

● Marijuana doesn't make people violent or aggressive like alcohol does.

● It seems to be less harmful than most drugs and is certainly less harmful than alcohol or tobacco.

WHAT I DON'T LIKE ABOUT MARIJUANA

● I seem to sit around doing nothing a lot.

● I spend too much money on marijuana.

● It's hard to tell whether things really are that funny if everything seems funny when you're stoned.

● I don't seem to have so many plans for the future.

● My circle of friends has gotten smaller and only seems to include others who smoke a lot of marijuana.

SEARCHING QUESTION
Sam (see panel on page 30) has been smoking marijuana for many years. At what point in his life do you think he became dependent on it? Do you think he realized it at the time, and do you think he considers himself dependent on it now?

Border Patrol agents question a group of illegal immigrants trying to cross into the U.S. from Mexico. Much U.S. marijuana comes from Mexico and other countries in Latin America, often transported by poor migrants.

Youth is a time of growing and maturing, mentally as well as physically. Most adults who are blown off course for a while because of marijuana have finished their education, which will help them find jobs. They can put their drug use behind them and get on with their lives.

Young people often lose that choice if they have been distracted from learning because of their use of marijuana. Finding the normal world boring and uninteresting is dangerous if that world involves preparing for exams that could shape the rest of a person's life. Without a degree, a young person can miss out on the career of his or her choice—or on changing from one career to another in later life.

More at stake

Young people face more immediate problems when they take marijuana. Adults usually know what they are taking, either because they have a marijuana supplier they trust or because they grow it themselves. Young people who might not even know what marijuana looks like have to trust whoever sells it to them. It might be incredibly strong, or it might be mixed with other drugs. Either way, the results could be terrifying.

What marijuana does to long-term memory is another big problem. People who smoke it may risk permanently harming their memory and their ability to learn.

The legal complications surrounding marijuana are also more serious for young people. If they are caught and get a police record related to marijuana, young people—with little or no work experience—will find it hard to get a job.

" I have seen very smart young men degenerate into a complete mess during a psychotic episode triggered by smoking skunk. "

Abu Al Rahman, London Region Officer of the Federation of Black and Asian Drug and Alcohol Workers.

" We've got two-thirds of young people using it now. They're using forms of the drug . . . in which the THC content, for example, is often unknown. They're using it in ways that are very risky, and we're not doing a good job of educating [them] about the risks. "

Professor Wayne Hall, Queensland University, Australia.

Using marijuana regularly makes it harder to play sports because it affects the body's ability to judge distance and movement.

SEARCHING QUESTION

Many reports and users' accounts say that taking marijuana over long periods of time plays tricks with and even damages people's memory. Can you think of reasons why such a result would be even more alarming for a young person than for an adult?

Many of life's big debates have enough uncertainty to make it hard to come up with an easy answer. The issue of marijuana, especially whether or not it should be made legal, is an ethical debate that has divided people for decades. Each side seems to be stuck in its view and is unwilling to judge the other side's argument fairly.

The argument against

Some people believe that any drug that changes the way people behave is dangerous and should be made illegal. In their view, marijuana poses many risks, including some that may be unknown. They say that legalizing marijuana and making it easier to buy would lead to all sorts of problems, both for the people who take it and for society. According to this argument, marijuana users would make poor parents, teachers, and leaders for the future because of their bored attitude and lack of motivation.

Canadians campaigning to legalize marijuana have replaced the maple leaf on their national flag with a marijuana leaf emblem.

> **Drugs to me is cocaine, heroin. Herb [marijuana] is the healing of the nation.**

Paul David, a Rastafarian living in New York, 1998.

FREEDOM OF RELIGION

Some religious groups use marijuana in their ceremonies. Rastafarians, for example, believe marijuana is holy and an essential part of worship. It is a sacrament, like the bread and wine that Christians take in Communion. Rastafarians in Jamaica argue that laws guaranteeing freedom of religion should allow them to use marijuana.

Americans in favor of such an approach point out that although all alcoholic drinks were illegal in the U.S. between 1919 and 1933, Christian churches were still allowed to use wine in their worship.

Some people say that governments could earn vast amounts of money from tax if marijuana were sold legally in the same way as cigarettes.

" I just want to know why I can't grow it in the privacy of my own home and smoke it in the privacy of my own home. I don't drink alcohol; I just want to take marijuana for my multiple sclerosis. That's all I ask. Please. "

Barry Clark, speaking at a debate entitled "Cannabis: Should it Be Decriminalized?" in London, December 11, 1997.

The argument for

Other people have a very different view. They argue that marijuana does not lead to violence and broken families in the way that alcohol can. Despite the evidence (see pages 24–27), they believe that, unlike tobacco, marijuana does not lead to medical complications. In short, they say that marijuana does not damage its users permanently and is a harmless way of relaxing.

They say that legalizing marijuana would remove the problem of not knowing exactly what is being sold. Government inspections could guarantee the quality of the marijuana sold, just as they guarantee other legal products, such as shampoo and vitamins. In addition, marijuana sold legally could be taxed, so governments could earn money in the process. As a result, criminals who deal in marijuana would probably go out of business.

Medical help

Supporters of legalization often quote its medical benefits. Marijuana has been used medically for centuries, mainly to relieve pain. In most countries, though, the drug remains illegal because governments have believed that legalizing marijuana for medical reasons would weaken marijuana laws in general.

Since the 1970s, though, many medical experts have come to support legalizing marijuana for some specific treatments. Evidence is mounting that THC, the active ingredient in marijuana, has real benefits in treating the eye condition glaucoma and the nerve disease multiple sclerosis (MS).

Glaucoma is a leading cause of blindness in many countries. Studies have shown that people with glaucoma felt less pressure (and pain) in their eyes after taking marijuana.

Multiple sclerosis affects people's nervous systems, causing pain and making movements difficult to control. Some people with MS have reported pain relief and easier movement after taking marijuana. Doctors cannot agree on whether these improvements are because of marijuana and, if they are, whether the drug could fully treat MS over a longer period.

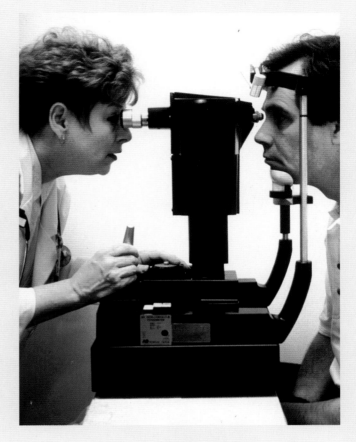

An eye specialist examines the eyes of a person with glaucoma. Some evidence suggests that marijuana can help treat this disease.

" Remember though that cigarettes are not new and novel. They've been abused for centuries. If the same thing were to happen with marijuana because of new freedoms, I'd be frightened. To put it mildly. I've seen what happens to people who think they know moderation. It's not at all pleasant. "

A post by balamm (blogger's name) on a filesharingtalk.com Web site in response to the question, "Will drugs become legal?"

SEARCHING QUESTION
Imagine that you were a politician who had just been elected to represent your country's government. Would you consider changing the laws on marijuana an important issue? Would you make it legal for everyone or only in certain medical cases such as for sufferers of multiple sclerosis and glaucoma?

A number of people in many countries believe that marijuana is harmless and should be made legal (see pages 34–37). Most people, though, believe either that marijuana is dangerous or that we don't know enough yet to be sure it is safe. This explains why the drug remains illegal, although the laws controlling marijuana (and how they are enforced) are constantly being studied and sometimes changed.

Elementary school students in the U.S., UK, Australia, and other countries now learn some of the basics about marijuana and other drugs.

Tough measures

Many schools in the U.S. operate a zero tolerance approach to marijuana and other drugs. Under this system, anyone found with marijuana in (or sometimes even near) a school is automatically expelled with no questions asked. This system has its opponents, but supporters say that students perform better and their education benefits as a result.

Other schools take a similar approach by testing students randomly for drugs. Faversham School in Kent was the first school in the UK to adopt this approach, beginning in January 2004. Twenty students, chosen at random, are tested at the high school each week. The school contacts the parents of anyone testing positive (showing traces of drugs), but only those who are known to be selling drugs are expelled.

The local police maintain a visible—yet friendly—presence at the Glastonbury Pop Festival, where marijuana use is common.

In August 2005, Faversham School published the results of the first exams taken under a full year of the new system. The results were better than the year before: 40 percent achieved good scores, compared with 26 percent in 2004. Principal Peter Walker believes that the random drug testing played a part in this improvement by helping students concentrate on their studies: "It has had an effect on contributions in the classroom and on behavior—with far less disruption and that sort of thing."

❝ The financial costs of policing marijuana amount to at least $90 million a year (including sentencing costs) and absorb the equivalent of 500 full-time police officers. ❞

From a 2002 report by the Joseph Rowntree Foundation, studying the cost of enforcing UK marijuana laws.

CLEAR AS MUD

Some countries, such as the UK (see page 41), have marijuana laws that apply nationally. Others, such as Australia and the U.S., leave much of the lawmaking (and enforcing) to state or regional governments. So the punishments for possessing marijuana can vary a great deal in one country. For example, in Australia in 2005, the maximum punishment for possessing three and a half ounces (100 g) of marijuana ranged from $115 (in South Australia) to 15 years' imprisonment (in Queensland).

The American position is even more complicated. In 2005, 10 states had laws allowing the use of marijuana for medical purposes. But U.S. federal laws do not allow this use of marijuana. The result is likely to be a lengthy battle in the courts to decide whether the states are free to enforce their own laws. In the meantime, millions of Americans remain confused about the legal position of marijuana.

A Cuban soldier stands guard over a large amount of marijuana that was confiscated from Jamaican drug dealers. The drugs will soon be transported to a secure site and burned.

New approaches

Many people who believe marijuana should remain illegal agree that using it is less serious than other illegal activities— robbery and assault, for example. They believe that the police could serve the public better by concentrating on these more serious crimes (and more serious drugs, such as heroin and cocaine) rather than using time and money to track down every marijuana user.

Some countries, especially the Netherlands, have long held this view and have decriminalized marijuana. It is still technically illegal to use marijuana,

although the police do not arrest anyone with less than an ounce (30 g) of the drug. The Dutch police also allow certain coffee shops to sell up to 0.18 ounces (5 g) of marijuana to people over the age of 18. Local or regional police forces operate similar policies in other parts of the world, such as Vancouver in Canada and Malaga in southern Spain.

Some coffee shops in the Dutch city of Amsterdam are allowed to sell small amounts of marijuana to customers who can only smoke inside the shop.

Changing the category

In the UK, the government classifies a drug depending on how harmful it is believed to be. Category (or Class) A drugs, such as heroin, cocaine, and LSD, are the most dangerous, and the penalties for selling and possessing them are the most severe.

In 2004, the UK changed the category of marijuana from B to C. The only real change is that the maximum penalty for possessing marijuana is reduced from five years in jail to two. First-time offenders under the age of 18 are taken to a police station for a formal warning in the presence of their parents or guardians. Later offenses can still lead to a conviction in the courts, which can prevent people from visiting some countries, including Australia and the U.S.

Taking marijuana can be a confusing and frightening experience, and the people you would normally turn to, such as close friends and family members, might not be able to help. Perhaps they think it is no big deal, or perhaps you have lost touch with your own family as well as older friends who don't smoke marijuana.

Other sources of help

Perhaps you are embarrassed to talk about using marijuana to family members or other people you know. Your school or local library will have books and brochures giving postal addresses and e-mail information for groups that specialize in providing advice and guidance.

Web sites are also worth looking at. Many web sites are run by international marijuana awareness organizations that often have branches near you. Marijuana Anonymous, for example, uses traditions of trust and cooperation to help people overcome their heavy use of marijuana. Just as importantly, it has information to help young people deal with heavy marijuana use by other family members.

The best support for young people can come from within the family if members are prepared to discuss marijuana and other difficult subjects freely.

Professional help

Medical professionals who have experience with alcohol and drug dependence can help people who have serious problems with marijuana. Private marijuana clinics are becoming more common in many countries, and some governments are building their own.

In 2003, the first of four marijuana clinics to be built by the Australian government opened in Parramatta, in southern Sydney. It has already proved to be a success. More than half of the people treated at the clinic have stopped using marijuana altogether (some had been spending $225 a week on marijuana); most of the others have cut down considerably.

" This is part of a comprehensive response the government's been taking to the emerging problem of links between marijuana use and marijuana overuse and various health, psychiatric, and social problems affecting young people. "

Australian Special Minister of State John Della Bosca speaking about the Parramatta marijuana clinic in Sydney, 2003.

Prince Harry of Wales went to Featherstone Lodge, a London drug treatment center, for a day in 2001 after his father learned he had smoked marijuana.

Glossary

administered given by a doctor or nurse

amotivational syndrome a mental condition in which a person loses interest in important things in life

amphetamines drugs that work on the body's nervous system to lift a person's mood

bronchitis painful irritation of the breathing passages

cash crop a plant grown because of the money it can bring in when harvested

cocaine a drug used in medicine as a painkiller and illegally as a way of boosting mood and confidence

dealers people who sell illegal drugs

depression a mental condition in which a person feels sad and unable to perform ordinary tasks

ecstasy an illegal drug that lifts a user's mood for several hours

emotions strong feelings such as excitement and sadness

expelled banned from school permanently

glaucoma an eye illness caused by increased pressure on the eyeball, sometimes leading to blindness

Hindi one of the main languages spoken in India

majority more than half of a group

malaria a disease causing chills and fevers, spread when mosquitoes bite humans

menstrual describing the monthly cycle of women of childbearing age; during the cycle, an unfertilized egg is shed with the uterus lining, which can cause painful cramps

moderation not doing something too much

multiple sclerosis a disease resulting from damage to the brain or nervous system, causing pain and loss of balance

opium an illegal drug that dulls the senses and sends people to sleep

paranoia the belief (because of a mental condition) that the outside world is hostile

peer pressure persuasion from people your own age to do something in order to remain part of the group

peers people of a similar age or social group

pneumonia a disease of the lungs leading to coughing, fever, and difficulty breathing

psychosis a mental condition that leads a person to lose contact with reality

Rastafarian a member of a religious group that originated in Jamaica and considers marijuana to be a holy plant

reclassified put in a different legal category

recreationally (in the case of drugs) taken for pleasure rather than for a medical reason

resin a sticky substance that comes from the sap of a plant

rheumatism the name given to several medical conditions that lead to swelling and stiffness of muscles and joints

sacrament a religious act that is a symbol of a person's beliefs

schizophrenia a severe psychosis that distorts a person's view of the real world

serrated having notches around the edges

strain a variety of a plant

tax a charge made by a government on income or on the sale of things

tincture a drug mixed with alcohol so that it can be drunk

withdrawal physical and psychological changes in a person who has stopped taking a substance after developing a dependence on it

World War I a global conflict, lasting from 1914 to 1918, involving many countries, mainly in Europe

Books

Connelly, Elizabeth Russell. *Through a Glass Darkly: The Psychological Effects of Marijuana and Hashish.* Philadelphia: Chelsea House, 1999.

Gottfried, Ted. *The Facts about Marijuana.* New York: Benchmark Books, 2005.

Kittleson, Mark, ed. *The Truth about Drugs.* New York: Facts on File, 2005.

Kuhn, Cynthia. *Buzzed: The Straight Facts about the Most Used and Abused Drugs from Alcohol to Ecstasy.* New York: W.W. Norton, 1998.

Lennard-Brown, Sarah. *Marijuana.* Chicago: Raintree, 2005.

McMullin, Jordan, ed. *Marijuana.* Detroit: Greenhaven Press, 2005.

Westcott, Patsy. *Why Do People Take Drugs?* Austin: Raintree Steck-Vaughn, 2001.

Web sites

Alberta Alcohol and Drug Abuse Commission
www.aadac4kids.com/thefacts/drugfacts/marijuana/index.asp
Provides information about marijuana and the effects of marijuana use.

Marijuana Addiction Treatment
www.marijuana-addiction-treatment.com
Offers information about marijuana addiction, as well as referrals to treatment centers.

Marijuana Anonymous
www.marijuana-anonymous.org
A Web site offering support to those who want to stop using marijuana.

National Institute on Drug Abuse
www.nida.nih.gov/MarijBroch/Marijteens.html
A fact-filled Web site about marijuana designed especially for teens.

National Institute on Drug Abuse for Teens
www.teens.drugabuse.gov/sarasquest/mj1.asp
Features a fun and informative quiz about marijuana and its effects.

Neuroscience for Kids
faculty.washington.edu/chudler/mari.html
Focuses on the effects of marijuana on the brain and nervous system.

Parents: The Anti-Drug
www.theantidrug.com/drug_info/drug_info_truth_mj.asp
Lists myths and facts about marijuana, as well as signs that someone you know may be using the drug.

Index